Cloud Song

Cloud Song

Poems by

Leslie Schultz

Kelsay Books

Cover: Leslie Schultz (2014)
Poet's photograph: Atia Cole (2017)

ISBN: 978-1-947465-59-6

Kelsay Books
Aldrich Press
www.kelsaybooks.com

This book is for Timothy Braulick—
love's champion, life's companion.

Acknowledgments

Grateful acknowledgment is made to the editors of the publications in which the following poems originally appeared (some in slightly different form).

Crossings: Poet-Artist Collaborations (XI, XII, & XVI): "Gilbert's Hobby," "Something in the Back," and "Nomad's Daughter"

Girlfriends Magazine: "Marriage Bed"

Light: "Consolation"

Mezzo Cammin: "Mozart at Age Five: Koëchel #1," "For My Daughter, Sleeping," "For My Daughter, Leaving Home," "Geography Lesson," and "Speed on to Spica"

Negative Capability: "Gilbert's Hobby"

Northfield Public Library: "Berry Fields in Snow"

Poetic Strokes Anthologies (2010 & 2011): "The Best I Have to Offer" and "Falling"

Stone Country: "Cloud Song" (titled "Cassatt: The Letter")

The Madison Review: "'Oh, Mrs. Miller!'"

The Midwest Quarterly: "April Exhilaration"

The Orchards: "Knot Garden," "Transportation," and "To a Former Friend, Whose Affection is Withdrawn" (nominated for a Pushcart Prize in 2017)

The Wayfarer: "The Botanical Guide to Select Poets of New England and New York"

Third Wednesday: "The Cannon City Creamery" "Nomad's Daughter"

Winona Media: (for National Poetry Writing Month—April 2016) "Yellow Slicker," "A Theory of Naming," "A Small Song for the Vast Mother," "Dark Oceans on Icy Worlds," "A Short Garden Report," Wisteria and Lattice Motif," "Vivid Tulips," "Uncaging the Bas," "Janus," "Three Haiku," and "Day Star" (also "Cruciferous")

Wisconsin Poets Calendar: "Twilight at Tenney Park"

"Triple Vision" and "Navigation" originally appeared, under different titles, in a chapbook, *Living Room* (Leslie Schultz Black, Midwestern Writers' Publishing House).

I am deeply grateful to my supportive circle of friends, family, and readers. Without your encouragement, I wouldn't have most of these poems. Your generous listening and your insightful comments are more valuable than you know. Thank you!

Contents

I. Little Paper Boats

Cloud Song

after "The Letter" by Mary Cassatt, 1890–91

for Sally Nacker

A page, a white island,
drifts on the jutting blue of the escritoire.
An envelope pressed to your lips
is likewise blank and dazzling,
though behind your shoulders
leaves rise and swoon like
a green calligraphy of birds,
and the shapes spilled on
your brocade jacket lock
with the intricacies of dragons
or dissolving clouds:
these hold you hesitant,
words forming and un-forming
behind your strong, black brows.

Sea Chanties

Essence of chanty
is synchronized breath—
singing together,
increasing our power
to do the work
that moves our ship
on the breath of the world.

Yellow Slicker

Niagara, New York, 1970

I put it on,
                and the floppy hat, too.
The arms hang way past my hands.
We each claim our place
                      at the railing—
Mom, clinging tight
                to squirrely little Kurt,
Karla, calm and watchful,
                          and Dad,
stowing his science fiction
                in a dry pocket.

Our sturdy tub
          begins to rock,
drawing nearer and nearer
                to the falls.
The approaching roar
          is like the vast silence
and heavy dark
          a mile under the earth
in Carlsbad Caverns.
                It was wet there,
too, but here,
          the whole world
is made of water

                    and the water
is singing,
          is pouring out
                  its stinging
notes,

needles
        made of mist,

each one
       a tempting siren
calling me closer
         to sounding adventure

the song of my life.

A Theory of Naming

...and from the shore
They viewed the vast, immeasurable abyss
Outrageous as the sea—dark, wasteful, wild.
   —John Milton, Paradise Lost (Book VII)

Dreaming, I was called
Batten-Down-the-Hatches!
Man-the-Pumps! and then
Dead-in-the-Water.

The world deems me Titanica,
riding the surface,
clueless
and fore-doomed.

Yesterday,
before I understood this,
I answered to Small Meadow
(Budded Tree, Cat-Mint, Field Lily).

Now I perceive my real name—
Sea Storm,
Tempest-Beneath-the-Waves.
I taste
of licorice and black tar.

Tomorrow I sink deeper,
becoming this:
Marianas,
Black-Smoker,
Sea-Vent,
Abyss.

Triple Vision

after "High Tide: The Bathers" by Winslow Homer, 1870

Three shadows on the sand.

The blonde bends toward shore.
Her hair waves loose,
Hides her face,
As she wrings out her skirt.
Droplets pelt the sand.

Her sister sits. Watches.
She flings a pebble from her shoe.
Her smooth head is level with the white
Cap of a breaking wave.

The other stands back,
Facing away from sisters and sea,
Wrapped in black. Her cap hides
Her hair. Perhaps she is blind. Her ear
Curves shell-like towards the others.

Unseen, a tiny sail of light speeds from the headland.

A Small Song for the Vast Mother

Earth Day, 2016

Fresh blows the wind on the mountain slope.
Fresh the green lace on the maple boughs.

Sweet the scent of the waking soil.
Sweet the sound of the glassy rain.

Deep the roots of the growing prairie.
Deep the fires in these ancient seas.

Here, we are cradled in moonlight and starlight.
Here, we rise with the traveling sun.

Now, we turn toward wisdom and insight.
Now, we see what must be done.

"Dark Oceans on Icy Worlds"

for Timothy

After days of clouds and spring rain,
sun pours through the dining room window,
filling translucent bowls of creamy porcelain.
Teacups—empty and clean—rimmed with gold,
are stacked askew like whirled orbits.

In the garden, one daffodil, a double-bloom
of peach and white, shakes its complicated folds
in as many directions as the wind
dictates, its whorls of petals predetermined,
like the swirling of galaxies, in patterns

noted by Fibonacci. (We count more easily,
apparently, because he also authored *Liber Abaci*
and championed numerals then called Hindu-Arabic
or *modus Indorum.*) Inspired by early travels,
this mathematical Leonardo used what he'd seen

in his youth to make his father's mercantile
woes ease, and meanwhile re-energized
medieval thought about the Golden Mean.
Now, seeing a headline from my husband's magazine,
Sky & Telescope, I wonder what it means

that I can travel simultaneously,
leaping past what numbers delineate,
(but respectfully, mindfully)
into speculative realms of astrobiology;
and thoughts of moon jellies at Monterey;

and of the wonder, in their tiny mock-sea,
of golden jellyfish who follow the sun daily
across their Palauan lake, like aquatic
sunflowers, turning away
from stellar cold and the merely shadowy.

Navigation

after "Boating" by Édouard Manet, 1874

Neither is quite at ease.
The sail is full. The oarsman
leans on the tiller,
tilts his straw boater to smile
at the lady. Her hat
is black and white. She
wears a veil and stares
at the rippling lights beyond
the sail. She does not watch
her sailor watching her, charting
the swell and fall of her blue dress.

Transportation

Spring in Faribault, Minnesota

for Karla Schultz

I come here now, to the seat of Rice County,
to sign and pay for my teen daughter's
passport. Soon, she'll study in another country,
perhaps along the Neva's storied waters.

On our meander home, I think of my own
first long journey, transported by my parents
to live with other immigrants in Melbourne—
slow Yarra River and wattle-tree fragrance,

shark nets at swimming piers, battered fish and chips.
Memories cascade as I go to the old
P.O. near the Cannon River's flow,
glimpse a Somali girl's garments billow,
step in to mail a card. One sound stops me cold:
frantic cheeping of hatched chicks—boxed—being shipped.

To a Former Friend, Whose Affections Are Withdrawn

I accepted you. You once enchanted me.
Now I accept that I'll never know your heart.
Yet how can friendship crumble into the sea?

You're older. I thought your wisdom was a key,
a mirror to illuminate my soul and art.
I accepted you. You once enchanted me.

I saw then that you're cantankerous, touchy,
sweet, kind, inclined to lob a verbal dart.
But can true friendship crumble into the sea?

You've hurled me into waves of uncertainty.
Did I wrong you? Did I bruise some tender part?
I accepted you. You once enchanted me.

You owe me nothing. I won't call. Don't worry—
Nothing unseemly will come from me. No retort.
I see our friendship sinking in the cold sea.

No matter. I've no taste for futility.
Trust has fled. Our affections are wrenched apart.
I must accept that you once enchanted me,
and now our friendship crumbles in a cold sea.

The Best I Have to Offer

I make my poems into little paper boats,
put a light in each, a small votive candle;
then sail them into the dark.

They are borne on my experience, over
shoals and snags, the salt and cold rot,
monsterous and sinuous beauty rocking deep beneath.

Poets always know that their fragile vessels
may never reach the other shore or
even see the morning, but
what else can we do?

Poems are precious,
and the light they carry is
the inestimable treasure of witness.

Together, flotilla of millions,
they form new constellations,
fling back radiance into the ocean of stars.

Sleep Ritual

for Lin and Bob Bruce

Say "hush" to the whole world:
the ravens, the traffic, the ocean tides, the humming
electric wires and flickering lights.

Say "hush" to your family;
kiss them and let them go.

Do not count sheep: let the whole flock
slip through the gate
into the dew-laden pasture.

Say "hush" to the roar of your own breath
sounding in your ears like the sea
inside a smooth, pink shell.

Calm the mad pumping
of your heart, that four-chambered nautilus,
that engine of your sea-worthy vessel.

Know you are nearly there,
gaining the shore
of the Kingdom of Sleep.

Step out of the small launch of your thoughts.

Allow your wet boots
to crunch through the surf and shingle;
climb to higher ground.

Plant your staff in the sweet grass;
let your mind unfurl
like a pennant of pure silk.

For My Daughter, Sleeping

Your hair, glowing
like fine Baltic amber,
spreads on your pillow.
In deepest slumber

what dreams will wash from
this oceanic night,
will nourish you before
dawn's shell-pink light?

Crossing the Briny Sea Like Some Evening Star

Three postcards lie on my table, tumbled
from personal and collective history, disparate, yet now
connected as row houses. A young man and a doomed queen.
She gazes at him across the arc of centuries,
across the curving Clachan Bridge, built to link Seil Isle
with land south of Oban.

Newly Henry's third queen, you sit, Jane Seymour,
for his painter, Hans Holbein, who captures
the small pouch under your young chin, soft as a mollusk.
He sees how you glide, meek, defended at court by stiff quilting,
by gilt bands framing the pulsing egg of your forehead, by jewels
and bland demeanor.

As he paints, the artist imagines you given to the aged royal bed—
unrobed, uncoiffed, unveiled—arrayed in only
a shift of thinnest lawn and your timid youth,
but bound by dynastic desires and fragile biology.
Planted with a son, you will deliver an heir, then
succumb to infection.

Now, fairy foxglove, *erinus plantaginaceae*, roots
frail purple colonists on a reflected stone eye,
a living garland mirrored in Atlantic waters.
This direction, west of Scotland, is not one
to which Henry looked until you died. His Plantagenet
mien bent most toward France.

But you, Jane, after nearly five hundred years, you
now catch a glimpse of your own sardonic Adonis,
lean-limbed, smiling, suited in a denim-azure haze.
Now your famed pallor warms with flushed roses.

Has your chaste shade been rendered susceptible
to Cupid's wayward dart?

It seems you lean forward. Loosed from the shackles
of temporality, your precise oil and tempera on oak
inclines westward toward his smeary pastels,
waves of blue and blond, shimmering and masculine.
Desirous, are you incited to tread this flowering masonry arc,
strong as a whale's back?

Listen! Across the wheezy hurdy-gurdy of Time itself
do you, too, hear the strains of a scruffy troubadour?
An angel with a mouth harp and a brigand's bandana
reels you in, invites you: "Won't you come see me,
Queen Jane?" Approximately your age, he offers plangent poetry,
sticky and delicious as love.

En Plein Air Ultramarine

When that morning sun bathes the silver shore,
cleansing the rocks and cockleshells of night,
you see him picking his way over more
uncertain ground, finding the right height.

In transit he looks ridiculous, weighted
with paint box, easel, a red folding chair.
At rest, he gathers dignity—a freighted
sea bird preferring its nest to the air.

All day, he will sit, anticipating,
facing the west, mixing a happy sunset,
ignoring his lunch on its napkin, waiting:
a pure tone of long ago indigo? a net

of clouds cast across the moon's coronet?
perhaps the lonely anguish of a star?
From dawn, he's poised to see what he will get,
trawling light with his canvas collecting jar.

The fishing boats are docked. You hear night squawks
of gulls. Far off, the painter closes his box.

II. Vivid Tulips

A Short Garden Report

for Ann Wilson Lacy

Days lengthen now, are softening.
Furzes and myriad greens screen sun
through a sieve of rustling.

Willows and pussy willows wave—
long lime-hued pennants down-spilling,
kitten-haloes at attention—

and even low-growing mosses,
emerging between these pink bricks,
send up thin flowers like flairs.

Wisteria and Lattice Motif

Here is what I remember:
hanging scallops of bloom—
articulated purple bells—
shook warnings we did not hear.

Floral rattlesnakes,
shaking so slightly
when we trod the board floors
of the rotting shotgun house.

So frail and decorative
they appeared, blanched
in moonlight, even as they
knocked ghostly knuckles,

even as they crushed
with their lush growth
the lattice supporting them.
I can hear them now,

sliding insistently
between frame and windowpane,
prising up nails, delicate
vegetal marauders.

Vivid Tulips

Can happiness by grasped by mind alone?
Here is a photo of me at age three,
knee-deep in drifts of tulips, a cast stone
thrown by joy into a vast floral sea,

waves of tulips bending to let me in.
I am swimming there, before memory
imprints or judgment alters direction,
so young I am content simply to be.

Sunbonnet askew, bare arms plunged in bloom,
the camera sees me gaze, dazed by glee;
no fine gradations of particular doom,
no thought beyond a present ecstasy.

Old photo, you're incomplete, like the mind's light,
so sharply focused in only black and white.

April Exhilaration

in praise of Northfield, in response to T. S. Eliot

Once again, spring has cast her lush magic,
her swaying net of red-gold shoots and tight
buds. Sleight-of-hand. Supreme conjurer's trick,
turning straw lawns wetly green overnight.

The sky goes oyster-grey, the weather wild.
A robin peers at its slick reflection
in a sidewalk pool and cocks its head, beguiled
by beak-flashes of curved, ochre direction.

Whatever is blooming unspools, spilling
colors like ribbons over the granite wall.
Wind crushes the new silk of the tulip, filling
its heart with the cardinal's scarlet call.

How quickly we forget the winter past!
April is cruel because it will not last.

My Neighbor is Wearing a Conehead

I hear a muffled sound, and so I look.
My neighbor is wearing a cone head. Yes.
Though it isn't Halloween.

At first, I am not sure
what I am seeing
behind the shrubbery; then her head emerges
crowned with a high dome of tan rubber: a hyperbole of a head.

She stands, waving the nozzle of a roaring leaf blower.

I don't mean to stare. But it's like wreckage on the highway,
only whimsical,
so startling I can't look away.

They aren't mad over there. They are artists.
They love colors. And herbs.
Once bubbles floated over the hedge
and kept coming for hours
strewn by a tiny machine made
of a fan and liquid soap.

I don't really know them.
I can't ask.
But I can't help wondering.

They give me hope.

Cruciferous

for Elizabeth Bishop

Silvered cabbages sparkle with dew,
appear like treasure in the field rows.

Peas twine along the chicken wire,
studded with fat purple blooms.
Sweet onions pulse toward the surface,
Their fragrant tops the green of park benches.

At the corner of my vision, a thin, black hose—
No! It's a snake weaving through the baby beets.
Raspberries glitter, cherries dance.
Asparagus has gone to seed, red berries bejeweling
those tops like fluffy Christmas trees, while corn silk
drapes wet, sweet, unripe.   A blush
of yellow-orange begins to gild the pumpkins
under the dragonfly-blue haze of August.

I think how this garden feeds my eye,
all of me, passes through me in many ways—death,
rot, renewal, and new fruit. I pick a nasturtium,
tuck it behind my ear, head up the hill, then pause—

there is a small rattling in the bluebird house.
Suddenly, the surprise of a rounded blue head, and
a rosy breast, flushed
like an embarrassed cheek or ripe peach:
duet tints of happiness.

Knot Garden

Portsmouth, New Hampshire

for JoAnn Kitzman Keen

I yearn for the old place called Strawbery Banke,
where buoys clang from the icy Atlantic

winter and summer. In May, a score or more
white houses open like shells, invite us

to pass through rooms lit by sun through wavy glass,
to wend from gate to gate through brick-lined gardens

where knots of healing herbs tumble and nod
in the salty wind. Strawberries grow low;

flower, leaf, and vine all at once with fruit;
later, leaves redden like berries, like sunsets

or the dawning of bad weather. Gardens,
Gordian, emblematic of all I

have not got, all I would slice through, for truth, but, failing,
build here, in the land of my own heart: fruit and paling.

Geography Lesson

In school, he misheard that Dallas is famous for rain.
In Minnesota, that morning, there was a light snow.
Then the radio spoke. His teacher wept in pain.

His brother told him that Airforce One is a plane,
That the president told the pilot where to go.
When young, he was sure that Dallas is famous for rain.

By noon, the sun shone on the president's campaign.
Mrs. Kennedy cradled red roses given for show.
Then the radio spoke. All the nuns wept in pain.

From his desk, he heard hungry crows in the corn complain.
On the playground, he kicked the ball toward a field row.
Just six, he believed that Dallas was famous for rain.

Their priest rushed from the sacristy like a freight train.
The Dallas sun shone now. Where was the promised rainbow?
The radio spoke. Sister Luke wept in pain.

The pilot's voice on the airwaves was tight with strain:
"The Angel is airborne." The plane was heavy with woe.
As a boy, he thought that Dallas was famous for rain.
The radio spoke. His mother kept weeping in pain.

The Botanical Guide to Select Poets of New England and New York

for Doris Kammradt

I.   *Robert Lowell*

A bird-of-paradise fluttering
in a cranberry bog.

II.   *Emily Dickinson*

Moss, lifting tiny, winged blooms,
on the north side of an etched tomb.

III.   *Robert Francis*

One purple clover is opening, still
as a stone on the stony hill.

IV.   *Robert Frost*

Maple boughs cast runic shadows
over the frozen, claw-colored earth.

V.   *Elizabeth Bishop*

Bougainvillea tumbles brilliantly
above the rusty gas pumps.

VI.   *Anne Sexton*

Blood-red roses, climbing,
almost escaping their thorns.

VII.   *Amy Lowell*

The green frog leaps,
skirts the alabaster lotus.

VIII.   *Wallace Stevens*

Against the granite façade, a singular blue
iris focuses the eye.

IX.   *Marianne Moore*

Yellow birch catkins, pendant,
tickle the cages of the wild things.

X.   *Edna St. Vincent Millay*

Magnolia, edged with cream,
arches, branching like candelabra.

XI.   *Sylvia Plath*

Tulips leaning, red and yellow,
toward a slash of white stucco.

XII.   *Maxine Kumin*

Ox-eye daisies reclaim the pasture,
marry sun with insight.

Falling

for Julia

Pregnant with you, I walked the Great Serpent Mound,
traced its spine with my feet on that last day
of its season, wound around the egg cradled
gently in its mouth. I did not know then
I carried you within me, tiny speck,
rocking between my pelvic bones as I climbed
the observation tower.
                              What did I see?
Ohio hills still shimmering with fall
though we were late into October, red
leaves vivid against the strong greens and golds,
and, far below, an opaque creek gliding
grey-blue and slow against the boles of trees.

I felt dizzy there, but dazzled. How could
I know how utterly you, with your copper
head, your quick smile and smell of buttermilk,
would transform me, pulling me down,
                                    down
through the gates of the underworld, alone
in the sounding dark until they cut you
from me and we rose together into the wet dawn
of July, clinging tight to each other,
memories of the fierce earth, unspoken
depths, binding us, new daughter, new mother.

Disturbances

My child, what would you have me say?
The maple leaves misrepresent
the agitations of this day.

Their green and golden shadows sway
lullabies while our hearts are rent.
My child, what would you have me say?

I carry with me all the way
deep into evening's discontent
the agitations of this day.

Can I adequately convey
how deeply—deeply—I repent?
My child, what would you have me say?

I trust, with time, one day, you may
review our words and be content,
but agitations fill this day.

I grieve to have to take away
a joy you held when innocent.
My child, what would you have me say
of agitations of this day?

Something in the Back

I dream I am making dinner
for my family, just
humming and chopping
and stirring, when,
from the back of the refrigerator,
I pull something I don't expect
or, at first, recognize:
the whole world,
not on a string
but on a stick
firmly attached to Antarctica.

Bigger than a lollipop
or beach ball,
it fills my kitchen
and my senses.

As I hold it, I notice
it is very sweet,
and it's dripping, and
it is in my hands.

My Environmentalist Daughter Plays
Pachelbel's "Canon"

And, again, her eyes close.

She plays this every day.
I see her upright body
slightly sway,
wince at an odd note,
keep on, an even tempo,
translate what Pachelbel wrote
into a bubble of sonic soap,
set it floating into each morning, this

hope

for our floating Earth,
harmonious climates, species rebirth—
mindful of dire warnings
but trusting, I suppose,
that humans must keep trying:

that to play is to recompose.

Uncaging the Bas

for Sally Nacker

It's a grey-again Sunday
after mere hours of honeyed sun,
two weeks of rain and wind,
three sudden squalls of snow.

Donning my long, grey coat,
taking up my shears,
I see what is emerging
and wish to help it grow.

Elizabeth Barrett Browning,
known at home as "Ba,"
had to escape her girlhood
in foggy London,

where she slept like
Sleeping Beauty,
to flower fully
in sun-kissed Italy.

You, tiny daffodils,
you bring her name each year
up from the winter snow,
and I must cut away

these dead stalks holding you
down, help you proclaim
openly, openly
your fragments of sun.

"Oh, Mrs. Miller!"

for Ellen Keller

"The baby's been crying
for half an hour,"
called the old neighbor
to the new mother
from behind the fence,
through the blooming roses
almost touching
the tear-soaked baby
in her carriage.

Beautiful, negligent
Mrs. Miller slid her long
feet into her shoes, left
her cigarette burning,
called her thanks, wheeled
the carriage from that farthest
garden corner back
to the little house,
hissing a little at the baby.

"Oh, Helen Rose," she fumed,
"grow up already,
why don't you?"
The wet baby, silent now,
absorbed the acrid smell
of the cigarette, the sharp
civet undernote of her mother's
scent, and failed to understand
her resentment, what it meant.

"Louie, Is That You?"

for Jane Pressel Schultz

The way I heard it,
it was in 1965, at a funeral in Grosse Pointe, Michigan.
My grandfather's brother and business partner, Uncle Ken,
had just buried his wife, Aunt Helene,
after a long battle with cancer.

The wind whipped in off the shore
of Lake Sainte Claire.
The neighbors came in, in twos and threes,
arms full of primroses or pot roasts, hats
in hand. Respect,
and showing it,
was the order of the day.

My mother was carrying coffee cups
into the Prussian blue dining room—
fine bone china—
when a distant neighbor, let's call him
Mr. Chiaroscuro, the one people whispered about,
was solemnly shaking hands
with Uncle Ken. Condolences came
formally from this man

who kept a plaster virgin in his garden,
a black-robed grandmother in his window,
who walked with elegance tinged
with violence, who was rumored to be
up to his neck in legitimate businesses and maybe
much more.

Then, Mr. Chiaroscuro glanced
across the room
and caught sight of Aunt Doris's husband,
standing between the potted palm and the credenza.

Startled, he barked, "Louie! What are you
doing here?"
Uncle Louie Bruno removed his hat, explained
this was family. His wife's family.

Mr. Chiaroscuro nodded, and soon went,
and, said my mother, everyone knew what it meant.

Gilbert's Hobby

He dreamed frequently of teeth
grown to the size of buildings,
pristine enamel
hung with ropes and men
busily polishing.

Lately, when he drove to the city,
the fence posts that held back the forests
with miles of bright wire
seemed to smile at him.

"Nature," his wife said, "is perfect,"
but he knew better;
he was trained to correct it.
Her teeth, for example. Without him
they'd still be clumped at random.
She had a nice smile now,
like a white picket fence.

His practice was thriving. Mostly ladies,
those with the trickiest mouths.
The trouble was
he could only help so many,
even on days when no one bit him,
and then, he could only fix so much.
Through all difficulties his patients
talked to him, exposed gaps
in their lives, their cleft marriages.

So, he'd murmur and neaten
what he could, then rinse his hands
and drive home to his hedges,

his wife's rampant garden,
and the warm, tiled room
with clean counters and sinks,
where he spent his evenings
twisting miniature trees.

Mother's Old Friends

for Jane Pressel Schultz

You ask if I remember Shirley Mullins,
your friend. Yes, but only dimly: just her
name, her husband (the mechanic,) her five
children with freckles and liver-colored lips.

I remember better Alice Kerr. Slim-hipped.
Mouthful of jangled teeth. Dark, curly hair
pinned into a pompadour. Forty-seven
then, Alice had wed a much younger man:

Connie. She helped him win his dreams
(arranging flowers, owning flower shops.)
On her science teacher's salary, with
the strong lacework of Bahai faith knotted

under her footsteps, she bopped and tangoed
to her own music. She called her musty house
"Moldy Manor". She called her hyperactive
little white dog "Peppy Locomotive".

She bathed in a claw-foot tub, all fretted
with rust, cheerfully sudsing herself no
matter who barged in (me, at seven) needing
to pee. Alice had sang-froid pumped by a

warm heart. When Connie sought a translation
of gender, they divorced but remained
friends. Really, we should name a new flower
for Alice: something spikey, sweet, tough, and rare.

Wandering Minstrel

I can see her
clearly
that nameless girl from fifth grade
with hair cut short like a boy.
She has blue eyes and pale skin
dusty with freckles. Her face is thin
and pointed, her teeth a little bit buck.
In this time of bell bottoms and love beads,
she wears a plaid cotton dress, short-sleeved,
painfully clean, with a wide collar.
Her skinny elbows jut out
under white cuffs.

We are both new to this school.
On the playground, she comes over to my group
with a smile and offers a song,
"The Red River Valley." She belts out
the cowboy tune with a funny tremolo
at the end of each note.
It sounds as though she
is pulling the song up from her toes
like a crop.

We giggle a little and thank her
and move away. We don't mean
to be mean, but we snicker.
We don't invite her
to join us at lunch.

I don't realize, not for years
and years, why she couldn't please:
a child without one ounce of shame –
Singing. Grounded. Herself. At ease.

Perfect

for Beth Dyer Clary

No. That will never happen, never
be achieved or conferred with magic
wands. Not perfection, not on any level.

Yet, the wish to perfect is ineradicable,
like buckthorn
in the heart. It crops up at the oddest moments.
Sometimes it dominates
mono-culturally, monomaniacally—

but somehow my attention always
wanders away
from ideas of crystalline obsession,
toward beauty—
sun slipping
behind the western trees, fish
tumbling in sparkles over the dam,
this garden in riots of color and seed.

I forget what I am not
and never will be, here
in this heartbeat,
in this lovely world,
and I remember
that I know it all to be very, very,
very good.

Tongues of Silken Fire

after "The Church Cat's Dream" by Derold Page, 1983

for Jan Rider Newman

Under mist that rolls like grey pearls over the hills,
she lies curled in sleep, comfortable among the stones
that mark where some sleep more greenly and deeply still,
that granitic repose, on hallowed ground, of bones.

Hearing the distant ringing of church tower's bell,
her pointed black ears twitch, though her eyes remain closed.
a fabulous dream tree grows taller with each knell,
and on every delicate branch a bird is posed.

Such birds! With feathers never seen in England Old
or New, like bits of rainbow clinging to each bough,
with songs unspooling from their throats, as bright and bold
as tongues of silken fire. What do cats know of sword or plough?

Let man or woman build a farm, a tomb, or poem.
Imagine the heavenly church cat, dreaming her way home.

Consolation

with a tip of the hat to Billy Collins

How agreeable it is not to be touring New England this autumn,
wandering her various cities shining on hills, nestling in vales.
How much better to watch the stalwart corn
brown in flat Midwestern fields, listen for the mouse rustling
in columnar acres of drying stalks.

There are no colonial thresholds here to cross.
no shadows cast by roofs with seven gables
or crimes of Puritans scourging human hearts.
No need to seek an acorn underneath
the Homestead's transcendent Amherstian oak.

How much better to catalog our garden's lovely weeds
than climb the hallowed staircase to The Mount
and count Wharton's vast achievements—with spare words,
with keenly sculpted landscape, with serene interiors.
We'll spend our time in silence, gathering seeds.

And why lament the loss of college visits
when down the street loom stony Gothic arches?
Don't Carleton's bells peal as sweet as William's?
And buildings at St. Olaf gleam, handsome and bespoke,
as any walls that cloister Mt. Holyoke?

Instead of boarding a silvery Amtrak train
and snoring as it licks the valleys up,
then hoping for a smoke-free rental car
and rented beds without the bite of bugs,
we can ground ourselves in joy, right where we are.

Let's settle here, my young, ambitious scholar,
and peep through college view books as leaves turn.
We'll just imagine how New England trees will burn.

Berry Fields in Snow

for Raymonde Noer

Rusted leaves flutter still, here and there,
like flags planted on arctic escarpments
at huge cost. Rarely, a scrap of jewel-
bright strawberry smolders, sooty ruby,
above the sparkle of new snow.
Across the road,
asparagus has gone to seed, taller
than ostriches, with nodding plumage
waving red-orange berries, like beaded fans;
and lean raspberry canes, tougher
than a miser's heart, arc
and crash over snow drifts.
Really, Hokusai
should be here with his paints, or Basho
with his pointed, bamboo brush.

Garden, La Louisiane, New Orleans

On the brown wall of my kitchen, hung in a black
certificate frame, an image of heaven is beckoning.

A row of diamond-squared tables advances
like a street: seven tables,
laid out for dinner, with cruets, and crystal goblets
overturned like bells, and
white linen from laundries where it never snows,
where steam rises from the river each evening,
where rain falls each afternoon
in drops large as tea cups.
Brown bentwood chairs are ready to draw out.
The lights strung above look hot,
shiny as peppers thrusting through the cool green
spikes of the potted palms.

Was it heaven in 1927? See the tropical red
and green of Christmas that year,
when Hank Somebody sent a two-penny writ
to Miss Clara E. in Denver,
and did not sign "Love." But sent a few words anyway,
poised on the image of an enchanted evening,
a magic dinner at La Louisiane.

Oh, may that be our common destiny!

Yet, more than years separate us
from that celestial reservation.
The glass in front of this picture is speckled, nearly
microscopically, with my own spaghetti sauce.

The chairs are smaller than fingertips. I listen,
but cannot hear the violins, the clatter of plates,
the low murmurs
of lovers as they choose
the perfection of anticipation.
No money changes hands. Somewhere,

the owner pushes back her black curls.
She fans herself, smiling. The stars are strung
in the heavens, burning and winking.
Steam rises from the jambalaya
like perfume.

Later, when the napkins are crumpled,
they will surely bring out the lemon ice.
With mint. Specialty of the House. Paradise.

III. Janus

Mozart at Five: Köechel #1

So complete, this deft-handed beginning:
delicate but assured. Fine bones.
Precise but varied as the world's spinning.

You can smell ambition. He's keen on pinning
down those faint, celestial tones.
Quite complete, his deft-handed beginning.

Young gambler, he's intent on winning
applause and love, those polished stones,
pretty and varied as the world's spinning.

The music of the spheres bows to him, keening—
harpsichord anticipates trombones.
So complete, this deft-handed beginning.

Composers know each note means re-beginning,
borrowing what one never owns,
precise but varied as the earth's spinning.

Like ladders, in his dreams come patterns leaning—
he dreams up sonic lattices and cones.
So completes this deft-handed beginning,
precise but varied as the world's spinning.

Perceiving Five Crows Aloft in a Lime Tree
on a Stormy Afternoon

Ragged wings, velvet
shadows, shuffle near
that green peak, sunlit.

Blue sky has darkened
to indigo, wind
has stilled now, but crows

contend louder than
thunder as it moves
across prairie grass.

Storm's ambassadors.
Sharp as ozone or
thorn, their calls roll

over the cut hay
into my inner-
ear, hammering on,

calling out in harsh-
throated gloating as
each piece of night falls.

Driving Through Rain

for Ellen Keller

The sweeping arm
of the rear-view wiper
slices through rain drops
like a metronome.

Reliable reaper,
it creates/recreates
one brief shape
of singing water.

A Palladian window,
open an instant
allows a glimpse
of the recent past.

Accelerating,
we travel through
dissolving tunnels,
collapsing time.

Marriage Bed

When you are away I could
move to the center, spread out like a star,
but I stay to one side, curled in,
just one-half of a whole heart.

Tang

for Timothy

There comes a turn in the weather,
a minor key.

The walnut's chevron fronds hang
golden over the grass.
Chartreuse fruits drop,
rinds rotting with the ease
of butter melting in midsummer.
Tannic shards spread stains
on the sidewalk where squirrels hunch,
fat and frantic, jaws pumping like pistons.

Too soon for that tang in the air—
wood smoke, those frost-dipped stars, harvest
moonlight silvering sheaves and snarls of drying beans.
But time for shoes and longer sleeves.
Sweater weather. A mild rain spangles
the purpling chrysanthemums and gilt yarrow.
One yellow leaf adorns the rusting wheelbarrow.

The Cannon City Creamery

Even more than a church, the creamery was the center of a small prairie town.
Prayers could keep, but milk turned sour.

May can be cold in Minnesota, damn
cold. One golden evening, coats buttoned to
the throat, we are stargazers on the lam,
Venus-eyed, searching for a clear west view,

and we roll the full length of Cannon City,
twenty houses, more or less, a few fields
strewn with auto parts and one pretty
barn wearing hub caps like shining shields.

Purple clouds hang near the partly budded trees
like smoke from some hidden, illegal fire.
Suddenly, over the remnants of prairie seas,
she sails into sight like sharp desire.

We wait, drawn over to the gravel ditch,
as lesser stars and planets stoke their lights,
turn reluctantly toward home. Then some itch
moves us toward a darkening shape. We're keyed-up kites,

driven before a stiff, historical wind.
The Palladian window is still clear, intact,
crowning the padlocked door like a diadem,
while under the cornice the bricks are stacked,

askew, looking as though a child pushed them
in, as if they might tumble in the next thaw.
This was the town center, a proud, civic hymn;
not even a buttery ghost now invokes awe

or pity, or stays the backward glance
that casts long shadows on all permanence.

Speed on to Spica

Here is a vexing truth I long to find:
(Is it a metaphor for my own mind?)
that streetlamp across the way, winking on
and off—all night, every night—at random…

Why shouldn't perceptions flux in clarity?
Breathe light in and exhale draughts of Lethe;
or, choking on some ancient Stygian gloom,
exhale insights to radiate the room?

Streetlamps are intermittently defective,
at times occasioning a choice invective
at damaged, city-managed circuitry.
Whom can I rail against to protest me?

My own mind a minor mystery. There we are:
not Arcturus. Just one quite variable star.

Janus

You know how it is. You see an image,
maybe two saguaro cacti leaning
toward each other, friendly, framing
a low orange sun. Automatically

you think "here is the southwest" because
Arizona is the famed state of the arid zone;
because the sun sinks just past it, nightly,
past the Golden Gate, into the sea.

Yet, can we trust such easy orientation?
This photo might have captured the just-rising sun,
if a dawn-treading photographer were pointing due east.
Objectivity can be quite blurry,

at times, depending on where we stand.
All we can know, certainly,
is that truth moves like the sun
and so, it seems, do we.

Three Haiku

for Karla Schultz

why do I keep them,
hawk feathers—gull, goose, and crow—
with sharpened pencils

glass jar—midnight blue—
a bouquet of soft feathers
and sharpened pencils

feathers or pencils—
which is most useful to me
who dreams of flying?

The Deep Well of Dreams

The work of night undoes the work of day.
Night unravels time and our intentions,
derails, by means of dreams, this lucid way.

We must careen toward the moon's inventions
and the flickering, sprocket-sprung motion
of the wandering stars whenever eyes
close or sun dips, liquid, toward the ocean
that reflects, dizzyingly, spinning skies.

It's not exactly rest to remove clothes,
put on pajamas, slide between the sheets,
and lay my head, like a luminous shell,
pulsing with wayward inclinations—woes,
desires—that have no place in daylit streets.

But I can't resist where sleep's whorls propel.

Agatha Christie at Work

I love to think of you sifting through
potsherds, carefully cataloguing broken bits
of lives shattered long ago.
You would have held the brush lightly, the fragment
firmly. The disillusioning dust of many ages—
encrusting the contours, disfiguring the design,
muddying the inscription—would have been no match
for your careful hands,
your patient heart, your clear eye.

In the unambiguous desert air, where
now drones patrol the dry rivers
and dusty bazaars,
you slacked your thirst
for order, for history, for
the struggle to make sense of the way
life smashes our assumptions, flings us
partial but still recognizable under its hooves.
I imagine the red sun sinking,

you, easing your shoulders, turning
your face to the currents of rising breeze.
A reliable evening, tidying the work tent,
admiring the silhouette of the tell
and your husband's loved profile.
The two of you retire, slipping into your tent,
quiet as fish. Later, you will light the lamp,
plumb the murderous depths of the human heart,
allow each piece of the mystery to slide into place.

New Spring

for Estelle Uleberg Swanson

In the small grocery co-op,
I see my friend's mother, age ninety-two.
She looks up at me, holding a cane
and a loaf of bread;
attentive, wizen, mouth agape,
eyes brightly curious as a new-born bird.

I cradle a carton of eggs,
smile and motion for her to go before me—
in line, out the door, into the greening world—
and she does, carrying the star-fire of her life
on her old swan's wings, leaning her way
up the hill despite a howling spring wind.

A White One

for Wallace Stevens

Not shy, this peacock with the red eye.

Young, feet planted in the spring mud,
he lifts the fresh fan of his feathers
high behind him, like a cloud of steam
rises from a cool morning lake,
like factory chimneys billow in the cold.

Omnivorous as moonlight, he drinks
in crashing sounds and stalks movement
in grasses—ants, crickets. He cries
hunger and triumph over new petals
and rattling seed. He cries his need.

All day, I ponder. Why?
Is he deformed or gifted, this ghostly
raucous bird with a ruby eye?
And can my winter-white page
hold a candle to his maker's rage?

Day Star

for Jan Rider Newman

Here in the dark, waiting
for the sun to proceed again
over the curve of the earth,
its daily round,
and hearing birdsong,
I understand: the whole world
waits, as we did.

I think of traveling to your house,
so long ago, visiting.
Our garden chairs were set beside
your red sub-tropical blooms,
the box of old negatives
at our feet, tea-dark strips of film
we layered into visors.

Laughing, we looked boldly
into the doubled dark
of that solar eclipse,
waiting,
certain as songbirds,
for the sun,
its radiant return.

Friendship is a Fragile Bird

that we cup in our two hands, wondrous.
We've hatched something together.
Now we hold it, feel it stirring,
try to protect our small hatchling from rough weather.

Yet existential cold presses, ponderous,
against these tiny curved claws,
bead-bright eyes. Hesitant wing-beats
knock staccato against its thin-ribbed heart.

How to let this bird rise in its moment,
release yet not abandon it,
let it follow its own life—perch—lift off
perhaps never to return?

We must be strong—for it and for us—cherish
the flame-shape it makes against the stars.

Scolded by Wrens

Summer lawn tumbles emerald velvet
under the fruiting crabapple's damask,
next to the splintered step ladder.
On both uprights we've affixed little painted houses
to attract the wrens, who do descend from sky and high

branches, begin to move in with industry.
They see us, but not our charity; they seem fused,
rather, by inhumanity, ruffled that humans think to share
the air nearby. A chair one meter
too close evokes full symphonies, tongue lashings

hatchings from genuine distress.
We think how light—how fragile—kind gestures
can be between us and species more free.
We think of those shattered Victorian greenhouses
built to shelter white orchids against the snow,
against their will.

Nomad's Daughter

I dream I see my father, once
the deluge is old news,
wandering in the street.
He has on his black,
zipped-up half boots and white socks.
Farther up,
blinding me, an immaculate
hospital gown, white
as the heart of a star.

He wears the stunned look
of the recently dead. A rime of salt
circles his open lips, but
he doesn't mind when I take him
by the hand, help him to lie down
right here, in the very center
of this poem.

Ice

for Corrine and Elvin Heiberg

Crossing the bridge, glancing left, to the north,
I brake and gasp. It cannot be, but is.
I couldn't be more amazed if two lithe
ballerinas in full tutus, toe shoes,
and tiaras lounged there on the thin ice
that partially clouds the dark turbulence
waters of the Cannon River.
Sun slants
like golden curtains
on a pair of swans,
escaped ornamentals but wedded fast.
Bridal white with black beaks, they curve against
the currents of air that separate
their slender throats, each holding up its own
heart-half, gesturing the shape of love,
as ephemeral—as vital—as breath.

For My Daughter, Leaving Home

I watch the inky soarings of one starling
against the rock-blue wall of falling night
and think how you, my lively, mortal darling,
are perched on your own edge of solo flight.

Night falls so many times to make a life.
Each new day one shimmering page must turn.
What will you seek? There will be hurt and strife,
but may you find what makes joy leap and burn

in your awakening heart, find help to know
why you were born on this sweet, fragile earth,
and how to make your mark, then let it go—
all of it, everything you've helped to birth—

allowing your dreams to flicker from your sight,
knowing they're borne up on their own delight.

Twilight at Tenney Park

While mallards tuck their green heads
beneath their wings to make their beds,
the willow's green and mournful arc
holds itself against the dark
resisting, as a reed will bend
before the wind, the twilight's end.

Reference Points

for Beth Dyer Clary

If even the bright stars change,
nightly, go swirling though
heaven from our point of view;
if stars are dying and are born;
if starlight, ancient—perhaps—
(can we know?) extinguished
long ago—then certainty
itself trembles. How are we
to comprehend when our small,
infinite, white-hot hearts burst
with fury and joy, pulse on
with determination, fall
into black holes of despair?

To chart possible progress
we must triangulate current
position, note past bearings
against the steady heartbeat
of infinity. Only
this offers any hope of
traveling with direction.

Yet how do we navigate
or steer when even the clear
heavens flux? This must be faith,
born in our bodies: to leap
across the divides of tide
and mind, staggering with our desire,
blind but still inclined
to live, which means to aspire.

The Spurwink Country Kitchen

for Timothy

We still talk about it.
It rose up like a mirage
on that November afternoon—
more than a year before our honeymoon—
a low white building with dove-grey eaves.

The narrow Maine roadway
dipped and curved through the spent
cranberry bogs. Its parking lot
was like a little oxbow lake,
a backwater.

We entered,
blowing on our cold hands, chose
a table near the big plate-glass window.
With one voice, we ordered coffee
and their homemade pie.

Waiting
for everything to arrive, we gazed out
at the red and dun bog plants
knee-deep in oyster-blue water; at the distant
tamaracks, stiff with golden needles
about to drop, or so we thought.

Where were we headed? It didn't matter.
Our compass was leisure. We speared forkfuls
of flaky crust as fogs rolled in, and were startled
to unusual alertness by bursting tart inky berries—
tiny as shad roe, bluer than unclouded summer oceans.

Surely the restaurant closed
a long time ago, but we still talk
about going back, ordering again
that perfect blue pie, holding hands, then
unfolding the map, driving off into that dazzling pearly sky.

Notes

Cloud Song is a collection of sixty-one poems that vary in formal structure and tone but are, as I see it, united by poetic voice, imagery, and theme. The first section, "Little Paper Boats," holds poems that employ watery imagery to explore travel across physical space and journeying through life. The second section, "Vivid Tulips," contains poems with botanical images that grow out of gardens, memories or images of flowers and nature, and the familiar ecosystem of the neighborhood. The third and final section, "Janus," looks in both of these directions—travel and growth, movement and rootedness—by using imagery of birds, sky and stars, and weather. Each poem is my attempt to convey perceived truth by precise imagery and attention to the music inherent in language. I hope that the result is a kind of beauty—not only of eye (image) and ear (sound) but also of clarity and hope.

Little Paper Boats

"Yellow Slicker" This poem combines two childhood vacation memories—the pounding silence and dark a mile under the earth in Carlsbad Caverns and the deafening roar of Niagara Falls heard from the deck of the famous Maid of the Mist excursion boat— with my long fascination with Yeats's poem "A Coat" (Responsibilities 1914).

"A Theory of Naming" A name is another kind of a coat. My given name, "Leslie," didn't seem to me to fit for many decades. In my mother's family the name is decidedly male (her father, brother, and nephew are all "Leslie."). As a child, I looked up the meaning of this Scottish-derived name, and the fit seemed even less "me". Various etymologies can be found, including "small meadow" (or "lea,") "garden of holly," or "from the grey fort." I wondered if I had a true name. Given the chance at age eight, for a week at camp, I asked to be called by my middle name ("Marie") and wore a necklace worked from string, bark, alphabet noodles and glue. That experience left me lonesome for my still-uncomfortable-to-me given name. In this poem, this hunt merges with the discomfort and empathy I felt as a young girl upon reading and rereading Hans Christian Andersen's story "The Little Mermaid."

Vivid Tulips

"A Short Garden Report" This poem celebrates looking closely and seeing what can be easily overlooked. As a tenth anniversary gift, my husband laid a brick patio in our back garden. Each year, the bricks shift, settle, and change hue. The cracks between are sometimes lush with various volunteer greens, including mosses and their delicate, antennae-like flowers.

"Wisteria and Lattice Motif" Two memories entangle in this poem. The memory of a beautiful living, marauding wisteria vine planted too close to an old house I once rented in Lake Charles, Louisiana is set against the more contained, two-dimensional silk working of wisteria on a Japanese Noh robe I saw in Philadelphia. The poem is propelled by oscillating ideas about beauty and danger, growth and destruction.

"April Exhilaration" My time and vista being different, Eliot and I perennially disagree about the nature of April's effect on the dead land.

"Cruciferous" This poem salutes the Community Support Agriculture (CSA) movement, a model in which consumers invest directly with farmers in the risks and rewards of small-scale organic farming. Tim, Julia, and I have been part of five different organic farms since the late 1980s, cherishing not only the produce but the relationships between people and with the land this way of intentional food production engenders.

"Falling" At one level, this poem is about how we fall in love with our children. It chronicles my first visit to Ohio's Great Serpent Mound with my Aunt Shirley when I was so newly pregnant that I did not yet know it. Five years, later, I returned with my husband, young daughter, and Aunt Shirley and her family to this powerful site. What is out of frame is how this maternal love leaves us open to the possibility of great pain when a child is sick, injured, or threatened by death (as codified in the Demeter-Persephone myths.) I wrote this poem during a sleepless night when my husband was out of town and my daughter, just a few months old, rolled over for the first time and fell off her changing table. Though a trip to the emergency room confirmed that no lasting damage was done, the reverberation of that moment of seeing her fall, of trying and failing to catch her as she tried out new power, has never left me.

"Perfect" This poem is inspired by Mary Oliver's poem ("Stanley Kunitz ") comparing the poet Kunitz in his garden—his self-described "poem that is never finished"—to the magician Merlin, and also by Ron Padgett's compelling collection of poetry entitled How to Be Perfect.

"Berry Fields in Snow" The piece of precious ground that gave rise to this poem, Lorence's Berry Farm, lies just north of Northfield, Minnesota on Foliage Avenue.

"Garden, La Louisiane, New Orleans" Sparked by an old hand-colored postcard I bought in a New Orleans book shop, this poem plays with concepts of paradise rising from the wall-garden depicted, the etymology of the word "paradise" itself, the hand-written note on the back of the card, and my memories of the incomparable fragrance and taste of food in the French Quarter: heaven, indeed!

Janus

"The Cannon City Creamery" Due to its proximity to the sun, Mercury isn't often visible. When it is theoretically visible, often such prosaic obstacles such as low-lying cloud bands, trees, or roof tops intrude. My husband and I have not yet managed it, but we still make the occasional star-gazing sortie. And we live in hope.

"Geography Lesson" My first inkling of the political realm came when I was three years old. That's when the Kennedy assassination and funeral dominated the news for many days. Cartoons were pre-empted—that caught my attention—and my parents tried to explain why. This poem uses the factual details of those horrific national events with my imagined account of the November 22, 1963 from the point of view of an eight-year-old boy attending a Catholic grade school bounded by cornfields, much like the one my husband attended in the tiny farm town of Searles, Minnesota.

"New Spring" The name "Uleberg" comes from the Norwegian for "howling mountain." Estelle Uleberg Swanson, the mother of my friend, Julia, is an inspiration to me. After this encounter at Just Food Co-op, I sat with Estelle and her daughter, Julia, in the kitchen of their family farmhouse near Madelia, Minnesota, and heard the story of how at just three years old Estelle scaled a nearby windmill. She frightened her parents but enjoyed the view! Her radiant and indomitable spirit continues to soar.

"A White One" On a trip to Lanesboro, Minnesota, I met an artist at their farmer's market who raises peacocks. In addition to jewelry fashioned from the usual iridescent colors, she had a number of pure white plumes from a young albino male in her flock. After learning that these albino peacocks exist, I began to wonder: what is the shape and hue of any essence? That question, combined with the image of the peacock, led (perhaps inevitably) to Wallace Stevens through his two masterful poems "The Idea of Order at Key West" and "Domination of Black."

About the Author

Leslie Schultz (Northfield, Minnesota) is the author of a collection of poetry, *Still Life with Poppies: Elegies* (Kelsay Books, 2016). Her poetry, fiction, and essays have appeared in a number of journals and anthologies, including *Able Muse*, *Light*, *Mezzo Cammin*, *Poetic Strokes Anthology*, *Swamp Lily Review*, *Third Wednesday*, *The Madison Review*, *The Midwest Quarterly*, *The Orchards*, and *The Wayfarer*; in the sidewalks of Northfield; and in a chapbook, *Living Room* (Midwestern Writers' Publishing House). She has twice had winning poems in the Maria W. Faust sonnet contest (2013, 2016). She is also the author of two works of middle-grade fiction set in fictional Sundog, Minnesota (Do Life Right Press); and is co-author (with artist Marilyn Larson) of *A Pocket Guide to* Labyrinths (Chronos Unlimited Press). In 2017, her poem, "To a Former Friend, Whose Affections Are Withdrawn," was nominated by *The Orchards* for a Pushcart Prize. Schultz posts poems, photographs, essays, and fiction on her website: www.winonamedia.net.

Kelsay Books

www.ingramcontent.com/pod-product-compliance
Lightning Source LLC
Chambersburg PA
CBHW071102090426
42737CB00013B/2435